WHERE AM I?

This is a watery place.
It is deep and dark.

WHERE AM I?

By Moira Butterfield

Illustrated by
Stephanie and Simon Calder

Thameside Press

Distributed in the United States by
Smart Apple Media
123 South Broad Street
Mankato, Minnesota 56001

Editor: Honor Head
Designer: Helen James
Illustrators: Stephanie and Simon Calder
Map illustration: Robin Carter / Wildlife Art Agency
Consultant: Steve Pollock

Printed in China

ISBN: 1-929298-36-6
Library of Congress Catalog Card Number: 99-73408

Where am I in the world?
Read this book
and see if you
can guess.

A squid lives here.
See if you can find
it in the pictures.

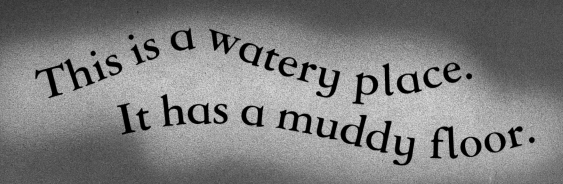

This is a watery place.
It has a muddy floor.

A sea cucumber crawls
along the bottom of the sea.
It sifts through the slimy
mud for food. It has little
lumps along its back.

Flat fish glide across the muddy floor. Sometimes they are the same color as the mud. That makes them hard to see.

Deep down it is dark and cold.

Many of the animals that live here are small and very fierce. They hunt each other for food. Some have lights on their heads.

The gulper eel can open its mouth very wide. It can swallow fish much bigger than itself.

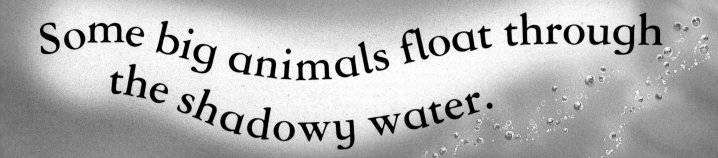

Some big animals float through the shadowy water.

A gray whale and
her baby are swimming
along together.
The mother whale is
as big as a truck.

The mother whale will care for her baby until it is as big as she is. They make different noises called whale songs.

Some fish swim in big groups called schools.

Lots of herring are swimming together. How many can you count? They have shiny, silvery scales.

Something with sharp
teeth is prowling here.
It is a hungry blue shark
looking for a mouthful
of tasty fish to eat.

There are rocks here. Fierce animals live among the rocks.

A moray eel peeks out of its den. Its long body is hidden inside. It has sharp teeth, and if it gets angry it will bite.

Can you spot a brown, bumpy stonefish hiding on the rocks? It has poisonous fins sticking out of its body. Watch out for a fierce hammerhead shark, too.

A forest of tall plants grows here.

The plants are seaweed.
Tiny fish called seahorses
live in the seaweed. They
have long, wavy tails.

A sea otter has found a spiky sea urchin. It will smash the urchin's shell with a rock and eat the soft insides.

Animals that look like plants grow on top of the rocks.

Can you see something with feathery branches, like a tiny tree? It is called coral. It looks like a plant, but it is an animal.

Can you spot a reef shark and
a turtle with a shell on its back?
The big, flat fish with a funny
face is called a manta ray.

Lots of corals growing together are called a reef.

Corals look very beautiful. They grow in many shapes and colors. Can you find a starfish in the coral?

Brightly colored fish live on a reef. How many different ones can you see? The animal with eight legs is an octopus.

Animals dive under the water to look for food.

Seals are good divers and swimmers, and they like to eat fish. This is a good place for them to find a meal.

Some birds are good divers, too. Under the water they grab fish in their long beaks.

The sun shines on top of this place.

Some animals have to put their heads above the water to breathe. The hungry bird flies off to eat its fish.

A round jellyfish floats in the water. It has long tentacles underneath, which can give a nasty sting.

Do you know where I am?

I am in the Pacific Ocean.

The Pacific Ocean is the world's biggest
ocean. It stretches halfway around the world,
and it is home to all kinds of animals.

This is a map
of the world.

There are oceans
all around the world.
The Pacific Ocean
is dark blue on
the map.

Pacific Ocean

I am here.

Pacific Ocean

Where are these animals?
Turn the pages back to find them.

Sea cucumber

Leafy sea dragon

Clown fish

Sea urchins

Stonefish

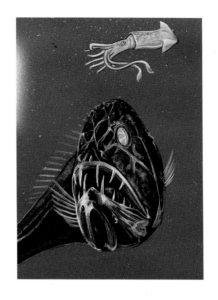

Fangtooth

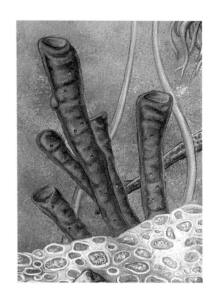

Glass sponges

Angelfish

Gulper eel

Dragonfish

Animal facts

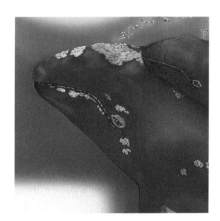

Some whales have small animals called barnacles clinging to their bodies. You can sometimes find barnacles on the beach.

The octopus can change the color of its skin to hide from enemies. It squirts ink from its body when it is attacked.

The anglerfish has a tiny bobble that shines like a light. Little fish swim toward the light and are gobbled up.

Most starfish have five arms, but some have many more. If an arm is damaged in an attack, they can grow a new one.

Sea turtles lay their eggs in the sand on beaches. When the baby turtles hatch, they crawl to the sea and swim away.

This sea bird, called a booby, is diving into the water to catch fish. Its feathers are covered in oil to make them waterproof.